THE AMERICAN EAGLE

The Symbol of America

THE
AMERICAN
EAGLE

The Symbol of America

*The bald eagle has
been the United States'
national symbol since
June 20, 1782.*

BY JON WILSON

GRAPHIC DESIGN
Robert A. Honey, Seattle

PHOTO RESEARCH
James R. Rothaus, James R. Rothaus & Associates

ELECTRONIC PRE-PRESS PRODUCTION
Robert E. Bonaker, Graphic Design & Consulting Co.

Library of Congress Cataloging-in-Publication Data
Wilson, Jon
The American Eagle : The Symbol of America / by Jon Wilson
p. cm.
Summary: Describes the history of the eagle as a symbol in other
cultures and how it came to be the national
symbol of the United States.
ISBN 1-56766-545-4 (library bound : alk. paper)

1. United States—Seal—Juvenile literature.
2. Bald Eagle—Juvenile literature.
3. Signs and symbols—United States—Juvenile literature.
[1. United States—Seal. 2. Bald eagle. 3. Eagles. 4. Signs and
symbols.] I. Title
CD5610.W48 1998   96338   98-5879
306.4 — dc21   CIP
                                                      AC

CONTENTS

A Nation Under the Eagle   7

Up in the Sky   8

The Legends   11

Family Crests   12

The Spirit Bird   15

The American Eagle   16

The Great Seal   19

The Eagle in Space   20

Commitment to the Eagle   23

Glossary & Index   24

A NATION UNDER THE EAGLE

For more than two hundred years, the eagle has been called a *symbol* of America. What is a symbol? It is something that represents something else. Letters are symbols that represent spoken sounds. Flags are symbols that represent countries, states, or organizations. Team colors and mascots are symbols that stand for sports teams. We use symbols in religion, in politics, and in many other parts of our lives. The eagle is a symbol of the United States that brings our country together just as our flag and our national anthem do.

People have used symbols for thousands of years. Animals have always been a favorite type of symbol. A country's national symbol is often an animal that represents the qualities most important to that country. Of all Earth's animals, few have been chosen as symbols as often as the eagle. The power, grace, and beauty of this bird have made it a perfect symbol for our country.

Eagles belong to a group of birds called **raptors.**
Raptors are birds of prey—birds that live by hunting
small animals. Hawks and owls are raptors, too.
Raptors live on most of Earth's continents. Eagles are
some of the most impressive of our planet's raptors.
They have excellent vision, powerful wings, and
sharp claws called **talons.** They soar high in the sky,
moving through the air with grace and skill. From
these heights they swoop down to grab their prey.
They are loyal, staying with one mate throughout
their lives. Eagles have come to stand for power,
loyalty, grace, speed, strength, and skill.

Right:
*A bald eagle swoops
down to catch a fish.*

Left:
*Bald eagles are
easiest to see when
they are sitting in
trees near rivers.*

THE LEGENDS

Through time, people have created many stories and legends about eagles. The people of Greece, the Middle East, India, Asia, Africa, and Europe all had legends about eagles. They told these stories to teach values such as strength, courage, and vision. Some of these stories were passed down from parent to child over hundreds or even thousands of years. The stories show people's deep respect for eagles.

A French print of "Thalia carried by the eagle Zeus" taken from an ancient Greek vase.

The Roman Empire adopted the eagle as its official symbol in 104 B.C. Troops of Roman soldiers marched behind the figure of an eagle carried on a pole. It was a great honor to be the person selected to carry the pole. The soldiers saw the eagle as a symbol of their army's strength and power. It gave them courage as they marched into battle.

FAMILY CRESTS

During the Middle Ages, many noble and royal families throughout Europe included eagles in symbols called **family crests.** Family crests were designs the families used to represent themselves and their heritage. The families placed their crests over their doorways and fireplaces and on their clothing. They carried the crests into battle on their armies' flags and on the shields of their knights, archers, and soldiers.

Many of these crests are still remembered as family symbols today. The study of family crests is called **heraldry.** People use the crests to help trace family histories. A family history, called a **family tree,** lists parents and grandparents and other relatives going as far back as information on them can be found. Some family trees go back several hundred years.

Four family crests using the eagle or parts of an eagle in their design.

THE SPIRIT BIRD

Left:
*The stylized figure
of an eagle tops a totem
pole in Stanley Park.
Vancouver, Canada.*

Right:
*A ceremonial dance
costume with the head of
a bald eagle on it from
the 1994 Yakima Indian
Nation Powwow in
Washington State.*

Long before Columbus or the Pilgrims came to
America, Native American peoples considered the
eagle to be one of the most sacred animals and a
powerful spirit. They used its feathers in important
ceremonies, to heal the sick, and to increase power
and strength. Finding an eagle feather was considered
a great honor—a gift from the spirits. Native
Americans viewed the eagle as soaring high above
the world and seeing everything in the heavens and
upon the Earth. Many Native American people today
still honor these beliefs.

THE AMERICAN EAGLE

In 1782 Thomas Jefferson, one of the founders of the United States, chose a kind of American eagle called the *bald eagle* as the new nation's symbol. On June 20, 1782, the nation's founders developed a design, called a **coat of arms,** that would appear on all official papers and in all government buildings. A coat of arms is a design that stands for a country, its people, and its government. William Barton, an expert on heraldry, helped the first Continental Congress decide on an appropriate design. Charles Thompson, the Secretary of the Continental Congress, developed the final design. This new coat of arms eventually became known as *The Great Seal of the United States of America.* At its center is the eagle.

An 1800 portrait of Thomas Jefferson, the third president of the United States of America, painted by Rembrandt Peale.

The Great Seal of the United States of America.

The Great Seal of the United States represents independence and freedom. The eagle at its center is shown holding objects in its talons and beak. On the right side, it's talons hold an olive branch with 13 leaves and olives. The olive branch symbolizes America's desire for peace, with the first 13 states shown as the leaves. On the left side, the eagle's talons hold 13 arrows, which symbolize America's willingness to protect its independence and freedom. The eagle's beak holds a scroll, or rolled paper, with the words *"E Pluribus Unum."* This phrase, which is in Latin, means "one out of many" or "one country from many states." It represents the 13 original colonies' joining to form one nation.

The eagle's grace and skill in flying made it the perfect symbol for the National Aeronautics and Space Administration (NASA). On July 16, 1969, when the first lunar lander gently came to rest on the surface of the moon, astronaut Neil Armstrong announced to the world, "The *Eagle* has landed." NASA had appropriately chosen the name *Eagle* for the first spacecraft to land humans on the moon. Even one star group, or *constellation,* is named after the eagle. It is called *Aquila,* the Latin name for the eagle.

The crest for the Apollo 11 Mission to the moon.

We see eagles used as symbols everyday—so often, in fact, that we are seldom even aware of it. The eagle of the Great Seal of the United States is featured on the back of the one-dollar bill. The United States Postal Service's symbol also features an eagle and is displayed on mailboxes and trucks all over the nation. Sports teams, such as football's Philadelphia Eagles, use the eagle as a symbol, too. The highest level in the Boy Scouts of America is the Eagle Scout. Branches of the United States military use the eagle to represent high rank, such as captain in the navy and colonel in the army. Even in golf, the term "eagle" is used for a feat of skill—playing a hole in two shots under par.

COMMITMENT TO THE EAGLE

Long before the United States became a nation, eagles soared everywhere across the continent. But more recently, pollution almost killed off these magnificent birds. An insect-killing chemical known as DDT was one of the main culprits. When eagles ate animals contaminated with DDT, the birds' eggshells got too thin for the babies to survive. In 1967, bald eagles were in such danger of dying out that they were listed as an **endangered species.** This listing gave bald eagles protection under the Federal Endangered Species Act.

A bald eagle soaring across a blue sky is a beautiful sight worth saving.

Quick action by scientists and the government seems to have saved the bald eagle. In fact, today the population of eagles in the United States is growing. In 1782, our nation's founders chose the eagle as our national symbol. It is up to all of us to make sure these magnificent birds continue to soar through our country's skies.

GLOSSARY

coat of arms (KOTE of ARMS)
A coat of arms is a design that represents a nation and its people and government. The United States's coat of arms, called the Great Seal, features an eagle.

endangered species (en-DANE-jurd SPEE-sheez)
An endangered species is a kind of animal or plant that is in danger of dying out. Bald eagles were an endangered species 30 years ago.

family crests (FAM-il-ly KRESTS)
Family crests are designs used to represent many European families. Many family crests include eagles.

family tree (FAM-il-ly TREE)
A family tree is a "map" of a family's history. It lists parents and grandparents and other relatives, sometimes going back for hundreds of years.

heraldry (HAIR-ell-dree)
Heraldry is the study of family crests.

raptors (RAP-terz)
Raptors are a group of birds, sometimes called birds of prey, that eat other animals. Eagles, hawks, falcons, owls, and vultures are all raptors.

talons (TAL-unz)
Talons are the long, sharp claws of a bird of prey. Eagles use their talons to hold and carry their dinner.

INDEX

Armstrong, Neil, 20
Barton, William, 16
coat of arms, 16
Continental Congress, 16
endangered species, 23
family crest, 12, 13
family tree, 12
The Great Seal, 16, 18, 19
heraldry, 12
Jefferson, Thomas, 16, 17
legends, 11
NASA, 20
Native Americans, 15
raptors, 8
Roman Empire, 11
symbol, 7
talons, 8
totem pole, 14